GAIL DUFF

ONE POT MEALS

HAMLYN

Produced by New Leaf Productions

Photography by Mick Duff
Design by Jim Wire
Typeset by System Graphics
Series Editor: James M. Gibson

Published by The Hamlyn Publishing Group Limited,
Bridge House, 69 London Road, Twickenham,
Middlesex, England.

First published 1987

ISBN 0 600 327043

Printed in Hong Kong by Mandarin Offset

We would like to thank:
Lurcocks of Lenham, The Square, Lenham, Kent; Brian
Cook and Son, Greengrocers, Charing, Kent; Honesty
Wholefoods, Union St., Maidstone, Kent; Jenny Hudson,
Karen Wood and Sandy Brown, Ceramics 7 Gallery,
7, Turnpin Lane, Greenwich, London SE10 9JA; Nasons
of Canterbury, 46/47, High St., Canterbury, Kent; and
Peckwater Antiques, Charing, Kent.

CONTENTS

INTRODUCTION

One-pot dishes can be many and varied. There are warming stews and casseroles, tender boiled meat with dumplings and thick and substantial soups, plus many other dishes in which the ingredients are prepared separately and then brought together for the final cooking of a delicious dish. That layer of mashed potatoes on a shepherd's pie or that crisp suet crust or that spiced scone topping can cover not only meat or beans but also vegetables as well. An enormous quiche can contain all the ingredients needed for a balanced meal, rice can be added to a stir-fried main dish and versatile pasta can be made into lasagne and other more quickly prepared dishes.

One-pot meals are also varied in character. They are not all substantial cold weather meals. Try, for example, Eggs and Avocado under Choux Pastry, or Pasta with Tuna, Lettuce and Cucumber, or one of the mixed salads.

Many one-pot meals are simple to prepare and to cook, involving fewer pans than usual and therefore less washing-up. Even those in which the ingredients are prepared separately can be made in advance, so that you can clear up the kitchen a long way ahead of your mealtime, leaving you with only one large dish to deal with after the meal. With all one-pot meals, there will be no sorting out of separate vegetable dishes at the time of serving. They will take up less room on the table and so are ideal for serving in small kitchens or even bed-sitters.

Besides all these advantages, one-pot meals are absolutely delicious. If the ingredients are chosen well, they will complement each other beautifully, sauces will moisten crisp toppings and the flavour of the main ingredients will permeate potatoes, rice and dumplings. If you have never tried it before, the one-pot technique will bring a wider variety of delicious meals to your kitchen.

Balancing the meal

When making a one-pot dish, you must include all the essential ingredients of a balanced meal. First of all there must be protein: meat, fish, eggs, cheese, pulses or nuts. You can have just one type, or you can mix them as in minced beef with kidney beans or fish with eggs. If you are basing a meal only on beans or nuts, always combine a whole grain product with it, such as a topping made with wholewheat flour, brown rice or wholewheat pasta. Combine the protein with two or more vegetables, so that you include essential vitamins and minerals. Then all you need is the carbohydrate, or filling, part of the meal. This can be potatoes, dumplings or suet crust, a scone topping, shortcrust or choux pastry, rice, another grain, or pasta. For extra goodness choose wholewheat flour and pasta and brown rice and other whole grains such as pot barley or buckwheat. These three basic types of ingredients will give you a completely balanced meal.

Basic cooking methods

Many different cooking methods are used in the following recipes, and all are designed to make the most of your ingredients. One of the mistakes that is often made when cooking one-pot meals is to add all the vegetables at the same time as the meat and consequently over-cook them to an unrecognisable mush. In many of the recipes, whether for boiled beef or paella, vegetables are added towards the end of the cooking time so that they keep a good colour, flavour and texture.

Kitchen equipment

The only essential pieces of kitchen equipment needed for making one-pot meals are large pots, pans and ovenproof dishes. Make sure before you start a dish that you have a container large enough. It is highly inconvenient to transfer all your ingredients to something larger when you are half way through a recipe. Ideally you should have at least one each of the following:

> large flameproof casserole
> large saucepan
> paella pan
> large ovenproof dish about 5 cm/2 inches deep
> large deep ovenproof dish
> large pie dish

Using a slow cooker

If you like to prepare your meals well ahead, many of the dishes are suitable for a slow cooker and this has been indicated at the end of the recipes. When using a slow cooker, turn it onto a high heat for the first 20 minutes of cooking time and then to a low heat for the remaining seven or so hours. Those cookers with an automatic setting will do this for you; thus it is best to read the manufacturer's instructions first. Also remember to use less water or stock than in a dish cooked in the oven or on the stove, and add it to the dish boiling. Pour away all excess fat after browning meat. Cut root vegetables into smaller pieces than the meat to ensure even cooking, and make sure that all dried beans have been rapidly boiled for 10 minutes and drained before being added to the dish.

Accompaniments to a one-pot meal

Since all the constituents of a balanced meal are already in the pot, no accompaniment is necessary. To add a touch of freshness, however, a green salad is always welcome. You can also begin the meal with a small salad starter.

Note: All recipes serve four people unless otherwise stated.

SOUPS

A warming soup can make a meal in itself and can take many forms from the substantial Peasant Soup with Spiced Dumplings to the lighter White Fish and Prawn Chowder which would be more suitable as a lunch or supper dish. Serve them all in big, deep bowls.

PEASANT SOUP WITH SPICED DUMPLINGS

1.4 litres/2½ pints stock
175 g/6 oz split red lentils
1 bay leaf
225 g/8 oz Chorizo sausage
1 large onion, finely chopped
1 garlic clove, finely chopped
pinch of cayenne
450 g/1 lb white cabbage, shredded
dumplings
225 g/8 oz potatoes
100 g/4 oz wholewheat flour
1 teaspoon baking powder
4 tablespoons olive oil
1 medium onion, finely chopped
1 garlic clove, finely chopped
1 teaspoon paprika

Put the stock, lentils and bay leaf into a saucepan. Bring them to the boil. Remove them from the heat and leave them for 1 hour.

For the dumplings, peel, boil and mash the potatoes. Beat in the flour and baking powder. Heat the oil in a frying pan on a low heat. Put in the onion, garlic and paprika and cook for 2 minutes. Mix them into the potatoes. Form the mixture into sixteen small balls.

Chop the Chorizo sausage. Put it into a saucepan and set it on a low heat. When the fat begins to run from it, put in the onion and garlic and soften them. Stir in the cayenne and cabbage. Add the stock and lentils. Bring them to the boil and simmer for 45 minutes, adding the dumplings for the final 20 minutes.

SIMPLE BEEF SOUP

for boiling

2.25 litres/4 pints water
1 carrot, roughly chopped
1 onion, halved, not peeled
1 celery stick, broken
1 leek, cut into 5-cm/2-inch pieces
1 teaspoon cloves
1 teaspoon black peppercorns
¼ teaspoon salt
bouquet garni
575 g/1½ lb topside or braising steak, in one piece

for finishing

225 g/8 oz carrots, finely chopped
225 g/8 oz leeks, finely chopped
4 celery sticks, finely chopped
100 g/4 oz mushrooms, finely chopped
450 g/1 lb potatoes, scrubbed, finely chopped
175 g/6 oz white turnips, finely chopped

Put all the boiling ingredients into a saucepan except the beef. Bring them to the boil. Add the beef, cover and simmer for 1½ hours, or until the beef is tender.

Remove and finely dice the beef. Strain and reserve the stock. Return the stock to the cleaned pan. Bring it to the boil. Put in the prepared vegetables. Cover and simmer for 15 minutes. Add the beef and simmer for a further 5 minutes.

Note: A slow cooker can be used for the first cooking of the beef.

THICK MINESTRONE SOUP

225 g/8 oz carrots
4 celery sticks
1 large onion
225 g/8 oz courgettes
1 green pepper
1 red pepper
3 tablespoons olive oil
1 garlic clove, finely chopped
450 g/1 lb minced beef
3 tablespoons tomato purée
3 tablespoons wholewheat flour
1.75 litres/3 pints stock
175 g/6 oz wholewheat spaghetti, broken
2 tablespoons grated Parmesan cheese

Finely dice all the vegetables. Heat the oil in a large saucepan on a low heat. Put in the carrots, celery, onions and garlic and cook them on a low heat for 15 minutes, stirring occasionally. Add the minced beef and stir for it to brown. Stir in the tomato purée and flour and then the stock. Bring the stock to the boil, stirring. Add the peppers and courgettes. Cover and simmer for 15 minutes. Add the spaghetti and simmer for a further 15 minutes. Serve in individual bowls with the Parmesan cheese sprinkled over the top.

Note: Suitable for a slow cooker.

PASTA AND TOMATO SOUP WITH EGGS AND CHEESE

900 g/2 lb tomatoes
450 g/1 lb runner beans, fresh or frozen
3 tablespoons olive oil
2 medium onions, finely chopped
1 garlic clove, finely chopped
4 tablespoons chopped parsley
2 tablespoons chopped thyme, or 2 teaspoons
    dried
2 tablespoons chopped marjoram, or 2
    teaspoons dried
2 tablespoons chopped basil, or 2 teaspoons
    dried
1.4 litres/2½ pints stock
175 g/6 oz small wholewheat pasta shapes
4 eggs
100 g/4 oz Cheddar cheese, grated

Scald, skin and chop the tomatoes. Slice the runner beans if they are fresh. Heat the oven to 200°C, 400°F, gas 6.

Heat the oil in a large saucepan on a low heat. Put in the beans, onions and garlic. Cover them and cook them gently for 5 minutes. Put in the tomatoes and herbs. Cover and cook for 10 minutes, or until the tomatoes are soft. Pour in the stock and bring it to the boil. Add the pasta and simmer, uncovered, for 12 minutes.

Divide the soup between four heatproof bowls. Break an egg into each bowl and cover it with the grated cheese. Put the bowls into the oven for 15 minutes.

GREEN LENTIL SOUP

225 g/8 oz aubergines
1 tablespoon fine sea salt
4 tablespoons sunflower oil
225 g/8 oz courgettes
1 green pepper
1 red pepper
2 medium onions
1 garlic clove, finely chopped
175 g/6 oz long-grain brown rice
225 g/8 oz green lentils
2 teaspoons paprika
600 ml/1 pint tomato juice
1.15 litres/2 pints stock
½ teaspoon Tabasco sauce

Finely dice the aubergines. Put them into a collander and sprinkle them with the salt. Leave them to drain for 20 minutes. Rinse them under cold water and dry them with absorbent kitchen paper. Finely dice the remaining vegetables.

Heat the oil in a large saucepan on a low heat. Stir in all the vegetables and the garlic. Cover and cook gently for 5 minutes. Stir in the rice, lentils and paprika. Pour in the tomato juice and stock and add the Tabasco sauce. Bring the soup to the boil, cover and simmer for 50 minutes, or until the lentils are soft.

Note: Suitable for a slow cooker

WHITE FISH AND PRAWN CHOWDER

fish stock
skin from 450 g/1 lb cod fillet
1 carrot, roughly chopped
1 celery stick, roughly chopped
1 small onion, roughly chopped
1 teaspoon black peppercorns
bouquet garni

soup
1 head celery
675 g/1½ lb potatoes
1 large onion
40 g/1½ oz butter
600 ml/1 pint milk
1.15 litres/2 pints fish stock
450 g/1 lb cod fillet
175 g/6 oz peeled prawns
1 (350-g/12-oz) can sweet corn
4 tablespoons chopped parsley

Put the ingredients for the stock into a saucepan with 1.75 litres/3 pints water. Bring them to the boil. Simmer, uncovered, for 30 minutes. Strain and reserve the liquid.

Finely chop the celery. Peel and finely chop the potatoes and the onion. Melt the butter in a saucepan on a low heat. Put in the celery, potatoes and onion. Cover and cook gently for 10 minutes. Pour in the milk and 1.15 litres/2 pints of the reserved fish stock. Cover and simmer for 30 minutes. Finely chop the cod. Add it to the soup and simmer for 5 minutes more.

Liquidise half the soup. Return it to the rest and reheat gently. Add the prawns, corn and parsley and just heat them through.

POTATOES

Potatoes are a welcome inclusion in any meal. Add them raw at the beginning of the cooking time or cook them and either layer them with other cooked ingredients for a final cooking or mash them to make a topping for a shepherd's pie. For a change choose sweet potatoes which have a flavour somewhere between ordinary jacket potatoes and chestnuts.

WINTER ROOT CASSEROLE

675 g/1½ lb stewing steak
675 g/1½ lb potatoes
350 g/12 oz carrots
350 g/12 oz swede
350 g/12 oz celeriac
1 large onion
25 g/1 oz butter
600 ml/1 pint bitter beer
600 ml/1 pint stock
2 bay leaves
2 tablespoons tomato purée

Heat the oven to 180°C, 350°F, gas 4. Cut the steak into 2-cm/¾-inch dice. Peel and dice the potatoes. Dice the carrots, swede and celeriac and thinly slice the onion.

Melt the butter in a flameproof casserole on a high heat. Put in the beef, brown it and remove it. Lower the heat. Stir in all the vegetables. Cover and cook them on a low heat for 10 minutes. Pour in the beer and stock and bring them to the boil. Add the bay leaves and tomato purée. Replace the beef. Cover the casserole and put it into the oven for 1½ hours.

Note: Suitable for a slow cooker.

IRISH STEW

675 g/1½ lb lean lamb
900 g/2 lb potatoes
450 g/1 lb carrots
6 celery sticks
2 large onions
6 tablespoons chopped parsley
salt and freshly ground pepper
1.15 litres/2 pints stock

Cut the lamb, potatoes, carrots and celery into 2-cm/¾-inch dice. Thinly slice the onions. Layer the lamb, vegetables and parsley in a large saucepan or flameproof casserole, seasoning well with pepper and lightly with salt as you go. Pour in the stock and add a little water if the stock does not quite cover the contents of the pan. Bring the stew to the boil on a medium heat. Cover and simmer for 1½ hours.

Irish stew is best served in deep bowls together with some of the broth from the pan. Any broth left over should later be used for a soup.

Note: Suitable for a slow cooker.

LIVER, GAMMON AND CARROT PIE

450 g/1 lb lamb's liver
25 g/1 oz wholewheat flour, seasoned
225 g/8 oz gammon steaks
25 g/1 oz butter
1 large onion, thinly sliced
300 ml/½ pint stock
4 sage leaves, chopped, or ½ teaspoon dried
  sage
1 tablespoon chopped thyme, or ½ teaspoon
  dried
450 g/1 lb shelled peas, fresh or frozen

topping
575 g/1¼ lb potatoes
450 g/1 lb carrots
50 g/2 oz cream cheese

Heat the oven to 200°C, 400°F, gas 6. For the topping, peel the potatoes and slice the carrots. Boil them together for 20 minutes or until they are soft. Mash them with the cream cheese.

Cut the liver into 2-cm/¾-inch dice and coat it in the flour. Dice the gammon. Melt three-quarters of the butter in a large frying pan on a high heat. Put in the liver, brown it quickly and remove it. Melt the remaining butter in the pan. Put in the onion and diced gammon. Cook them until the onion is soft, stirring frequently. Pour in the stock and bring it to the boil. Replace the liver and add the herbs and peas. Simmer, uncovered, for 2 minutes.

Transfer the liver mixture to a large, deep dish. Cover it with the potato and carrot mixture. Make patterns on top of the potato and carrot with a fork. Bake the pie for 30 minutes, or until the top is lightly browned.

PORK, LEEK AND APPLE CASSEROLE

675 g/1½ lb lean pork, cut from the hand, leg or shoulder
675 g/1½ lb leeks
675 g/1½ lb potatoes
1 crisp dessert apple
1 large onion
2 tablespoons sunflower oil
1 teaspoon mustard powder
300 ml/½ pint stock, boiling
150 ml/¼ pint dry cider, boiling
4 sage leaves, chopped, or ½ teaspoon dried sage

Heat the oven to 180°C, 350°F, gas 4. Cut the pork into 2-cm/¾-inch dice and the leek into 2-cm/¾-inch slices. Scrub and dice the potatoes. Core and slice the apple. Thinly slice the onion.

Heat the oil in a flameproof casserole on a high heat. Put in the pork, brown it and remove it. Lower the heat. Put in the apple and onion and cook them for 5 minutes, stirring occasionally. Mix in the potatoes and scatter in the mustard powder. Cook, stirring, for 1 minute. Add the stock and cider and bring them to the boil. Put in the pork and leeks. Add the sage. Cover the casserole and put it into the oven for 1¼ hours.

Note: Suitable for a slow cooker.

SMOKED FISH AND POTATO BAKE

675 g/1½ lb potatoes
2 green peppers
1 red pepper
1 medium onion
25 g/1 oz butter
450 g/1 lb smoked cod or haddock
300 ml/½ pint milk
1 bay leaf
1 slice onion
1 teaspoon black peppercorns
4 tablespoons chopped parsley
4 eggs, beaten

Heat the oven to 200°C, 400°F, gas 6. Scrub the potatoes and cut them into 2-cm/¾-inch dice. Steam them for 25 minutes or until they are just tender.

Core and seed the peppers and cut them into 2.5-cm × 6-mm/1-inch × ¼-inch strips. Thinly slice the onion. Melt the butter in a saucepan on a low heat. Put in the onion and cook it for 2 minutes. Put in the peppers, cover and cook gently for 10 minutes.

Skin the fish. Put it into a saucepan with the milk, bay leaf, onion slice and peppercorns. Cover and set it on a low heat. Bring the milk to the boil. Gently poach the fish for 2 minutes. Lift out the fish. Strain and reserve the milk.

Cut the fish into 2-cm/¾-inch pieces. Mix it with the potatoes, parsley, peppers and onion. Put the fish and vegetables into a shallow ovenproof dish. Gradually stir the reserved milk into the beaten eggs. Pour the mixture over the fish and potatoes. Put the dish into the oven for 25 minutes or until the custard mixture is set and the top is just beginning to brown.

HERRINGS FOR SUPPER

4 medium herrings
2 teaspoons made English mustard
900 g/2 lb potatoes
1 green cabbage
1 large onion
1 large cooking apple
6 sage leaves, finely chopped, or ½ teaspoon
    dried sage
2 tablespoons cider vinegar
salt and freshly ground black pepper
300 ml/½ pint tomato and vegetable juice
25 g/1 oz butter, plus extra for greasing

Heat the oven to 180°C, 350°F, gas 4. Fillet the herrings. Spread each fillet lightly with the mustard. Roll it up. Scrub and thinly slice the potatoes. Shred the cabbage. Thinly slice the onion. Peel, core and slice the apple.

Put half the potatoes into the bottom of a lightly greased casserole. Then put on half the cabbage, half the onion and half the apple. Put the rolled herring fillets on top. Sprinkle them with the sage and the cider vinegar. Season lightly. Put on the remaining apple, then the onion, cabbage and finally the remaining potatoes. Pour in the tomato and vegetable juice. Dot the top of the potatoes with the butter.

Cover the casserole and put it into the oven for 45 minutes. Remove the lid and continue cooking for a further 30 minutes, or until the top is brown and the potatoes are cooked.

Note: Suitable for a slow cooker.

CHEESE, POTATO AND CELERY PIE

900 g/2 lb potatoes
1 head celery
1 large onion
100 g/4 oz back bacon
25 g/1 oz butter
3 tablespoons wholewheat flour
1 teaspoon mustard powder
300 ml/½ pint milk
50 g/2 oz Gruyere cheese, grated
100 g/4 oz Cheddar cheese, grated

Heat the oven to 200°C, 400°F, gas 6. Peel and slice the potatoes, chop the celery and thinly slice the onion. Boil them together for 15 minutes, or until they are only just tender. It is best if they can keep their shape, once cooked. Drain them.

Finely chop the bacon. Melt the butter in a saucepan on a low heat. Put in the bacon and cook it for 2 minutes. Stir in the flour and mustard powder and then the milk. Bring the resulting sauce to the boil, stirring. Take the pan from the heat.

Mix the two cheeses together. Beat two-thirds of the cheeses into the bacon sauce. Carefully fold in the potatoes, celery and onion. Put the mixture into an ovenproof dish. Scatter the remaining cheese over the top.

Put the dish into the oven for 25 minutes, or until the top is golden brown.

SWEET POTATO STEW

900 g/2 lb lean pork, from the leg, hand or
    shoulder
675 g/1½ lb sweet potatoes
2 large red peppers
450 g/1 lb tomatoes
450 g/1 lb okra
25 g/1 oz lard
2 medium onions, thinly sliced
1 garlic clove, finely chopped
1 tablespoon paprika
¼ teaspoon cayenne
150 ml/¼ pint dry white wine
150 ml/¼ pint stock
6 sage leaves, chopped, or ½ teaspoon dried
    sage
pinch of salt

Cut the pork into 2-cm/¾-inch dice. Peel the sweet potatoes and cut them into 2-cm/¾-inch dice. Core and seed the peppers and cut them into strips, 2.5 cm × 6 mm/1 inch × ¼ inch. Scald, skin and chop the tomatoes. Slice the okra, removing the stalks.

Melt the lard in a saucepan or flameproof casserole on a high heat. Put in the pork, brown it and remove it. Lower the heat, stir in the onions and garlic and soften them. Add the peppers and okra. Cover and cook for 5 minutes. Stir in the paprika and cayenne. Add the tomatoes, cover again and cook for a further 5 minutes until they are soft. Pour in the wine and stock and bring them to the boil. Put in the pork, sweet potatoes and sage and season with the salt. Cover and cook gently for 45 minutes.

Note: Suitable for a slow cooker.

DUMPLINGS AND HATTED DISHES

Dishes with dumplings, whether casseroles or slightly lighter dishes of boiled meat, are real cold weather food. Hatted dishes consist of previously cooked casseroles put into a dish under a 'hat' of suet crust or other type of crust which is more substantial than ordinary pastry. Both small dumplings and 'hats' can be flavoured with herbs or spices, and the dumplings deliciously soak up the flavour of the dish.

VEGETABLE BAKE WITH WALNUT DUMPLINGS

225 g/8 oz haricot beans, soaked and cooked
350 g/12 oz aubergines
1 tablespoon salt
450 g/1 lb tomatoes
2 green peppers
4 tablespoons olive oil
1 large onion, thinly sliced
1 garlic clove, finely chopped
2 tablespoons chopped thyme or 2 teaspoons dried
dumplings
175 g/6 oz walnuts
75 g/3 oz wholewheat flour
pinch of salt
75 g/3 oz fresh wholewheat breadcrumbs
1 tablespoon chopped thyme or 1 teaspoon dried
1 teaspoon bicarbonate of soda
2 eggs, beaten

Dice the aubergines. Put them into a collander and sprinkle them with the salt. Leave them to drain for 20 minutes. Rinse them under cold water and dry them with absorbent kitchen paper. Scald, skin and chop the tomatoes. Core and seed the peppers and cut them into strips 2.5 cm × 6 mm/1 inch × ¼ inch.

Heat the oven to 180°C, 350F, gas 4. Heat the oil in a saucepan on a low heat. Put in the onion and garlic and soften them. Mix in the peppers and aubergines. Cover and cook for 5 minutes. Add the tomatoes, cover again and cook for 5 minutes more. Mix in the thyme and haricot beans and take the pan from the heat.

To make the dumplings, grind the walnuts in a blender or food processor. Mix them with the flour, salt, breadcrumbs, thyme and bicarbonate of soda. Bind the mixture together with the beaten eggs. Form it into sixteen small dumplings.

Put the vegetable and bean mixture into an ovenproof dish and put the dumplings on top. Put the dish into the oven for 30 minutes or until the dumplings are firm.

RED BEAN BAKE WITH SAUSAGE DUMPLINGS

225 g/8 oz red kidney beans, soaked and cooked
2 tablespoons sunflower oil
1 large onion, thinly sliced
1 garlic clove, finely chopped
575 ml/1 pint stock
2 tablespoons tomato purée
2 teaspoons molasses
2 tablespoons red wine vinegar
¼ teaspoon cayenne
1 large green cabbage, shredded
1 small head celery, diced

dumplings
225 g/8 oz wholewheat flour
1 teaspoon salt
1 teaspoon bicarbonate of soda
¼ teaspoon cayenne
100 g/4 oz vegetable margarine
125 ml/4 fl oz cold water
225 g/8 oz sausage meat

Heat the oven to 180°C, 350°F, gas 4. Heat the oil in a flameproof casserole on a low heat. Put in the onion and garlic and soften them. Add the stock, tomato purée, molasses, vinegar and cayenne and bring them to the boil. Add the cabbage, celery and beans and simmer for 10 minutes.

For the dumplings, put the flour, salt, bicarbonate of soda and cayenne into a bowl and rub in the margarine. Bind the mixture to a dough with the water. Form the dough into sixteen portions. Divide the sausage meat into sixteen portions and form each one into a ball. Completely enclose it in a portion of the dumpling mixture. Place the dumplings on top of the beans, cabbage and celery. Put the casserole into the oven, uncovered, for 45 minutes, or until the dumplings are firm. Serve straight from the casserole.

Note: The beans, cabbage and celery can be first prepared in a saucepan and then transferred to an oven-to-table serving dish for the final cooking with the dumplings.

CHICKEN AND LEEKS WITH LEEK DUMPLINGS

one 1.575 kg/3½ lb roasting chicken
12 prunes
275 ml/½ pint hot, strong black tea
1 lemon
2 teaspoons ground turmeric
bouquet garni
450 g/1 lb carrots
450 g/1 lb leeks
4 tablespoons chopped parsley

dumplings
225 g/8 oz wholewheat flour
½ teaspoon salt
½ teaspoon bicarbonate of soda
100 g/4 oz beef suet
4 tablespoons chopped green part of leek
200 ml/7 fl oz cold water to mix

Soak the prunes in the tea for 1 hour. Pit and chop them. Cut the rind and pith from the lemon and finely chop the flesh. Mix it with the prunes. Use this as a stuffing for the chicken. Stuff and truss the chicken and rub the turmeric into the skin. Place the chicken in a large casserole or saucepan and pour in cold water to come to the top of the legs. Add the bouquet garni. Set the pan on a medium heat and bring the water to the boil. Cover and simmer for 1 hour 10 minutes. Slice the carrots and cut the leeks into 2.5-cm/1-inch pieces.

For the dumplings, put the flour, salt, bicarbonate of soda, suet and chopped leek into a bowl. Mix them well and bind them together with the water. Form the dough into sixteen small balls. Twenty minutes before the end of cooking time, add the carrots and leeks to the pan and float the dumplings on top. Cover again and simmer gently until the chicken is done.

To serve, carefully lift out the dumplings with a perforated spoon and keep them warm. Lift out the chicken, carve it and arrange it on a serving plate with the stuffing. Scatter the parsley over the top. If there is room, surround it with the dumplings and vegetables. If not, add one or two dumplings and just enough vegetables to give the dish colour, putting the rest into separate dishes. Spoon a little of the broth over the top to moisten the chicken and serve the rest separately in a jug.

Note: Suitable for a slow cooker.

BOILED LAMB WITH CAPER SAUCE AND CAPER DUMPLINGS

for boiling
knuckle end of a leg of lamb weighing about 1.8 kg/4 lb
water to cover the lamb
2 tablespoons tarragon vinegar
bouquet garni, including 1 tarragon sprig and 1 mint sprig or 2 teaspoons each of the dried herbs
1 small celery stick, 1 small carrot split lengthways and 1 small leek, tied together
1 medium onion, peeled, left whole
freshly ground black pepper

vegetables
450 g/1 lb carrots
450 g/1 lb French beans

dumplings
225 g/8 oz wholewheat flour
pinch of salt
1 teaspoon bicarbonate of soda
100 g/4 oz beef suet
1 tablespoon chopped capers
4 tablespoons chopped parsley
200 ml/7 fl oz cold water

sauce
25 g/1 oz butter
2 tablespoons wholewheat flour
450 ml/³⁄₄ pint reserved stock
2 tablespoons chopped capers
4 tablespoons chopped parsley

Put the boiling ingredients except the lamb into a large saucepan or flameproof casserole. Bring them to the boil, cover and simmer for 10 minutes. Add the lamb. Cover and simmer for 1½ hours.

Quarter the carrots lengthways and cut them into 2.5-cm/1-inch pieces. Trim the French beans and tie them into four equal-sized bundles.

For the dumplings, put the flour into a bowl with the salt, bicarbonate of soda, suet, capers and parsley. Mix well and make into a dough with the water. Form the dough into sixteen small balls.

Twenty minutes before the end of the cooking time, remove the bouquet garni and flavouring vegetables from the pan. Put in the carrots and French beans and float the dumplings on top. Cover and continue cooking until the lamb is done. Carefully lift out the dumplings with a perforated spoon and keep them warm. Remove the lamb. Lift out the vegetables and keep them warm. Carve the lamb, arrange it on a serving dish with the vegetables and dumplings and spoon a little of the stock from the pan over the top. Keep it warm. Some dumplings and vegetables may be served separately if there is insufficient room on the dish.

For the sauce, melt the butter in a saucepan on a medium heat. Stir in the flour and a measured amount of stock from the pan. Bring them to the boil stirring. Add the capers and parsley and simmer for 2 minutes, stirring. Serve separately in a warm dish.

Note: Suitable for a slow cooker

BOILED BEEF AND CARROTS WITH CARROT DUMPLINGS

1.25 kg/2½ lb salted silverside or brisket of beef
6 cloves
10 black peppercorns
bouquet garni which includes celery leaves
2 bay leaves
4 medium onions, peeled and left whole
450 g/1 lb carrots
1 small white cabbage

dumplings
225 g/8 oz wholewheat flour
pinch of salt
1 teaspoon bicarbonate of soda
freshly ground black pepper
pinch of ground cloves
100 g/4 oz shredded beef suet
100 g/4 oz carrots, finely grated
150 ml/¼ pint cold water

Soak the beef overnight in cold water. Drain it. Put it into a large saucepan and cover it with fresh water. Add the cloves, peppercorns, bouquet garni, bay leaves and onions. Bring the beef to the boil on a medium heat and skim it if necessary. Cover and simmer for 1½ hours. Cut the carrots into lengthways quarters and then cut each piece in half. Cut the cabbage into eight lengthways wedges.

For the dumplings, put the flour into a bowl with the salt, bicarbonate of soda, pepper, ground cloves, suet and grated carrot. Mix well and form into a dough with the water. Form the dough into sixteen small pieces. Twenty minutes before the end of the cooking time, put the carrots and cabbage into the pan and float the dumplings on top. Cover again and continue cooking until the beef is done.

Lift out the dumplings and keep them warm. Carve the beef and put it onto a large serving dish. Garnish it with some or all of the dumplings and vegetables, depending on the size of the dish. Spoon a little of the broth from the pan over the top and serve the rest separately in a jug. Put any remaining vegetables and dumplings onto a separate dish.

Note: Suitable for a slow cooker.

BEEF WITH CARAWAY DUMPLINGS AND CABBAGE

900 g/2 lb stewing beef
1 green cabbage
450 g/1 lb tomatoes
25 g/1 oz butter
1 large onion, thinly sliced
1 garlic clove, finely chopped
1 tablespoon paprika
½ teaspoon caraway seeds
600 ml/1 pint stock

dumplings
225 g/8 oz wholewheat flour
½ teaspoon salt
1 teaspoon bicarbonate of soda
1 teaspoon paprika
1 teaspoon caraway seeds
100 g/4 oz shredded beef suet
200 ml/7 fl oz water
2 tablespoons tomato purée

Heat the oven to 180°C, 350°F, gas 4. Cut the beef into 2.5-cm/1-inch dice. Shred the cabbage. Scald, skin and chop the tomatoes. Melt half the butter in a flameproof casserole on a high heat. Put in the beef, brown it and remove it. Lower the heat. Put in the onion and garlic and soften them. Stir in the paprika and caraway seeds, cabbage and tomatoes. Pour in the stock and bring it to the boil. Cover the casserole and put it into the oven for 1¼ hours.

For the dumplings, put the flour into a bowl with the salt, bicarbonate of soda, paprika, caraway seeds and suet. Mix the water with the tomato purée and add it to the flour mixture to make a dough. Divide the dough into sixteen portions. Twenty minutes before the end of cooking time, put the dumplings on top of the beef and cabbage. Cook, uncovered, for the remaining time.

Note: Suitable for a slow cooker.

STEAK AND KIDNEY UNDER A HAT

675 g/1½ lb steak and kidney
4 tablespoons wholewheat flour, seasoned
225 g/8 oz open mushrooms
225 g/8 oz white turnips
1 small head celery
40 g/1½ oz butter
1 large onion, thinly sliced
600 ml/1 pint stock
2 tablespoons Worcestershire sauce
1 bay leaf
1 tablespoon chopped thyme
2 tablespoons chopped parsley

hat
225 g/8 oz wholewheat flour
2 teaspoons mustard powder
1 teaspoon dried thyme
½ teaspoon salt
1 teaspoon bicarbonate of soda
100 g/4 oz shredded beef suet
150 ml/¼ pint water

Heat the oven to 180°C, 350°F, gas 4. Dice the steak and kidney if necessary (it is often bought ready diced). Coat it in the seasoned flour. Thinly slice the mushrooms, cut the turnips into 2-cm/¾-inch dice and the celery into 2-cm/¾-inch pieces. Melt 25 g/1 oz butter in a large saucepan on a high heat. Put in the steak and kidney, brown them and remove them. Lower the heat, add more butter if necessary, put in the onion, mushrooms, turnips and celery. Cover them and cook gently for 5 minutes. Add the stock and bring it to the boil. Add the Worcestershire sauce and herbs. Replace the steak and kidney. Transfer the contents of the pan to a large pie dish. Cover them with foil and put them into the oven for 1¼ hours.

For the 'hat', put the flour into a bowl with the mustard powder, thyme, salt, bicarbonate of soda and suet. Mix it to a dough with the water. Roll the dough out so it exactly covers the pie dish. Put it on top of the steak and kidney mixture and return the dish to the oven for a further 20 minutes so the 'hat' becomes firm and just begins to colour. Serve straight from the dish.

Note: The steak and kidney mixture can be initially cooked in a slow cooker.

BEANS AND BRUSSELS SPROUTS UNDER A NUTTY HAT

225 g/8 oz pinto beans, soaked and cooked
450 g/1 lb Brussels sprouts
450 g/1 lb parsnips
1 large onion
25 g/1 oz vegetable margarine
300 ml/½ pint tomato and vegetable juice
300 ml/½ pint vegetable stock
¼ nutmeg, grated, or ¼ teaspoon ground
    nutmeg

hat
225 g/8 oz wholewheat flour
½ teaspoon salt
½ teaspoon bicarbonate of soda
100 g/4 oz vegetable margarine
25 g/1 oz Brazil nuts, ground
25 g/1 oz hazelnuts, ground
150 ml/¼ pint water

Heat the oven to 180°C, 350°F, gas 4. Trim the Brussels sprouts. Core and dice the parsnips. Thinly slice the onion. Melt the margarine in a saucepan on a low heat. Put in the onion and soften it. Stir in the Brussels sprouts, parsnips and beans. Pour in the tomato and vegetable juice and stock and add the nutmeg. Bring them to the boil, cover and simmer for 5 minutes.

For the 'hat', put the flour into a bowl with the salt, and bicarbonate of soda. Rub in the margarine. Mix in the nuts. Form the mixture into a dough with the water. Put the vegetables and beans into a large pie dish. Roll out the dough to exactly fit the dish and place it over the top. Put the dish into the oven for 30 minutes, or until the 'hat' is firm and just beginning to brown.

COBBLER DISHES

A cobbler dish consists of a stew of meat or beans with a scone mixture, usually in portions, baked on the top so that it soaks up some of the juices. The scone can be quite plain or flavoured with herbs or spices.

SPICED CHICKPEA COBBLER

225 g/8 oz chickpeas, soaked and cooked
450 g/1 lb courgettes
1 red pepper
1 green pepper
4 tablespoons sunflour oil
1 large onion, thinly sliced
1 garlic clove, chopped
1 teaspoon ground cumin
1 teaspoon curry powder
1 teaspoon paprika
300 ml/½ pint tomato juice

cobbler topping
225 g/8 oz wholewheat flour
½ teaspoon salt
½ teaspoon bicarbonate of soda
½ teaspoon ground cumin
½ teaspoon curry powder
½ teaspoon paprika
75 g/3 oz vegetable margarine
150 ml/¼ pint natural yogurt

Heat the oven to 200°C, 400°F gas 6. Thinly slice the courgettes. Core and seed the peppers and cut them into strips 2.5 cm × 6 mm/1 inch × ¼ inch. Heat the oil in a saucepan on a low heat. Put in the onion and garlic and soften them. Add the courgettes and peppers. Cover and cook for 5 minutes. Stir in the cumin, curry powder and paprika. Add the chickpeas. Pour in the tomato juice and bring it to the boil. Put the mixture into an ovenproof dish.

For the cobbler, put the flour into a bowl with the salt, bicarbonate of soda and spices. Rub in the margarine and bind the mixture to a dough with the yogurt. Form the dough into eight scones and place them on top of the chickpeas. Put the dish into the oven for 20 minutes or until the cobbler top is firm. Serve straight from the dish.

LAMB AND LEMON COBBLER

675 g/1½ lb lean lamb, from the leg or shoulder
450 g/1 lb small white turnips
350 g/12 oz carrots
1 large onion
2 tablespoons sunflower oil
300 ml/½ pint stock
2 tablespoons chopped parsley
1 bay leaf
juice of ½ lemon
100 g/4 oz watercress, chopped

cobbler
225 g/8 oz wholewheat flour
pinch of salt
freshly ground black pepper
1 teaspoon mustard powder
1 teaspoon bicarbonate of soda
grated rind 1 lemon
1 tablespoon chopped thyme or 1 teaspoon
   dried
1 tablespoon chopped parsley
75 g/3 oz butter
1 egg, beaten
9 ml/3 fl oz milk

Heat the oven to 180°C, 350°F, gas 4. Cut the lamb into 2-cm/¾-inch dice. Cut the turnips into 2-cm/3/4-inch dice and slice the carrots and onion. Heat the oil in a large flameproof casserole on a medium heat. Put in the lamb, brown it and remove it. Lower the heat. Put in the turnips and onion and cook them, uncovered, for 5 minutes, stirring occasionally. Add the carrots. Pour in the stock and bring it to the boil. Add the herbs and lemon juice. Cover the casserole and put it into the oven for 1 hour.

For the cobbler, put the flour into a bowl with the salt, pepper, mustard powder, bicarbonate of soda, lemon rind and herbs. Rub in the butter. Make a well in the centre and add the egg and milk. Mix everything to a dough. Form the dough into eight scones. Transfer the lamb to an ovenproof dish. Mix in the watercress. Heat the oven to 200°C, 400°F, gas 6. Place the cobblers on top of the lamb. Put the dish into the oven for 20 minutes, or until the cobblers are firm and beginning to brown.

Note: The lamb can be initially cooked in a slow cooker.

SAUSAGE CIDER COBBLER

675 g/1½ lb pork sausages
675 g/1½ lb leeks
25 g/1 oz butter
1 tablespoon wholewheat flour
150 ml/¼ pint stock
150 ml/¼ pint dry cider
1 teaspoon made English mustard
4 sage leaves, chopped, or ½ teaspoon dried
   sage

cobbler topping
225 g/8 oz wholewheat flour
½ teaspoon fine sea salt
½ teaspoon bicarbonate of soda
1 teaspoon mustard powder
½ teaspoon dried sage
75 g/3 oz soft lard
150 ml/¼ pint buttermilk

Heat the oven to 200°C, 400°F, gas 6. Grill the sausages until they are browned and cooked through. Cut them into 2-cm/¾-inch pieces. Cut the leeks into 2-cm/¾-inch pieces and steam them for 20 minutes or until they are just tender. Melt the butter in a saucepan on a medium heat. Stir in the flour and then the stock and cider. Bring the mixture to the boil, stirring. Beat in the mustard and sage. Fold in the sausages and leeks and transfer the mixture to an ovenproof dish.

For the cobbler, put the flour into a bowl with the salt, bicarbonate of soda, mustard powder and sage. Rub in the lard and mix everything to a dough with the buttermilk. Form the dough into eight scones and place them on top of the sausages and leeks. Put the cobbler into the oven for 20 minutes, or until the scones are firm and beginning to brown.

MINCED BEEF, BEANS AND BROCCOLI WITH A POTATO COBBLER

100 g/4 oz brown kidney beans, or pinto beans
450 g/1 lb broccoli or calabrese
450 g/1 lb tomatoes
225 g/8 oz mushrooms
1 large onion
4 tablespoons olive or sunflower oil
1 garlic clove, finely chopped
450 g/1 lb minced beef
2 tablespoons chopped thyme, or 1 teaspoon dried
2 tablespoons chopped marjoram, or 1 teaspoon dried
4 sage leaves, chopped, or ½ teaspoon dried sage

cobbler
675 g/1½ lb potatoes
½ teaspoon salt
25 g/1 oz butter
65 g/2½ oz wholewheat flour

Soak the beans and cook them until they are soft. Cut the broccoli or calabrese into small florettes and steam them for 20 minutes or until they are just tender. Scald, skin and chop the tomatoes. Thinly slice the mushrooms and onion. Heat the oil in a large saucepan or flameproof casserole on a low heat. Put in the onion and garlic and soften them. Add the beef and stir until it browns. Add the tomatoes, mushrooms, herbs and beans. Cover and simmer for 20 minutes.

For the cobbler, peel the potatoes. Boil them until they are tender and mash them with the salt and butter. Work in the flour to make the mixture into a soft dough. Form the dough into eight round scone shapes.

Put half the meat and bean mixture into an ovenproof dish. Put all the broccoli on top and cover it with the remaining meat and beans. Put the scones on top. Bake the cobbler for 25 minutes, or until the scone topping is firm and beginning to brown.

PIES

Shortcrust pastry is not in itself substantial enough to act as the main filler part of the meal, yet by putting your ingredients into a pie crust, you can cut down on the amount of potatoes, for example, that you will need. The chicken and the bean pies below make substantial main meals. The other two, which are more like quiches, can also be served cold for lunch or supper and are ideal for packed lunches.

CHICKEN, PARSLEY AND VEGETABLE PIE

for boiling
1.15 litres/2 pints water
1 onion, roughly chopped
1 carrot, roughly chopped
1 celery stick, roughly chopped
bouquet garni
1 teaspoon black peppercorns
675 g/1½ lb chicken breasts

for pie
225 g/8 oz shelled peas, fresh or frozen
350 g/12 oz carrots
450 g/1 lb potatoes
1 (350-g/12-oz) can sweet corn kernels
25 g/1 oz butter
2 tablespoons wholewheat flour
450 ml/¾ pint reserved stock
25 g/1 oz parsley, chopped
shortcrust pastry made with 350 g/12 oz wholewheat flour
1 egg, beaten

Put the boiling ingredients into a saucepan and bring them to the boil. Put in the chicken breasts, cover and simmer gently for 30 minutes. Take out the chicken breasts and dice them. Strain and reserve the stock.

Heat the oven to 200°C, 400°F, gas 6. Cook the peas in lightly salted boiling water for 10 minutes. Drain them. Dice the carrots and the potatoes. (The potatoes may be left unpeeled). Steam the carrots and potatoes together for 25 minutes, or until they are just tender. Drain the sweet corn.

Melt the butter in a saucepan on a medium heat. Stir in the flour and 425 ml/¾ pint of the reserved stock. Bring them to the boil, stirring, and simmer for 2 minutes. Take the pan from the heat and mix the parsley, vegetables and chicken.

Line a 25-cm/10-inch square, 5-cm/2-inch deep ovenproof dish with about two-thirds of the pastry. Put in the chicken filling and cover it with the remaining pastry. Seal the edges and brush the top with the beaten egg. Bake the pie for 30 minutes, or until the top is golden brown. Serve hot.

BLACK-EYED BEAN AND ROOT VEGETABLE PIE

225 g/8 oz black-eyed beans, soaked, cooked
   for 20 minutes, drained
350 g/12 oz carrots
350 g/12 oz swede
350 g/12 oz parsnips
450 g/1 lb potatoes
1 large onion
25 g/1 oz butter or vegetable margarine
300 ml/½ pint tomato juice
300 ml/½ pint stock
2 tablespoons preserved grated horseradish
2 tablespoons chopped thyme, or 1 teaspoon
   dried
4 sage leaves, chopped, or ½ teaspoon dried
   sage
100 g/4 oz watercress

pastry
275 g/10 oz wholewheat flour
pinch of sea salt
2 teaspoons paprika
100 g/4 oz butter or vegetable margarine
75 g/3 oz Cheddar cheese, grated
cold water to mix
1 egg, beaten

Dice the carrots, swede, parsnips and potatoes. Finely chop the onion. Melt the butter in a saucepan on a low heat. Stir in all the vegetables. Cover them and cook them gently for 10 minutes. Add the tomato juice and stock and bring them to the boil. Add the horseradish, thyme and sage and the beans. Cover and simmer for 20 minutes, or until the beans are soft. Take the pan from the heat. Chop the watercress and mix it into the vegetables and beans.

Heat the oven to 200°C, 400°F, gas 6. To make the pastry, put the flour into a bowl with the salt and paprika. Rub in the butter or margarine and toss in the cheese. Mix to a dough with cold water. Roll out about two-thirds of the pastry and line a 25-cm/10-inch square, 5-cm/2-inch deep ovenproof dish. Put in the vegetable and bean filling. Cover it with the remaining pastry. Seal the edges and brush the top with the beaten egg. Bake the pie for 30 minutes, or until the top is lightly browned. Serve hot.

HAM, EGG AND VEGETABLE PIE

450 g/1 lb leeks
450 g/1 lb potatoes
1 small head celery
350 g/12 oz cooked lean ham, in one piece
shortcrust pastry made with 275 g/10 oz
    wholewheat flour
225 g/8 oz low-fat soft cheese
1 teaspoon made English mustard
4 eggs, beaten
4 tablespoons chopped parsley
6 small streaky bacon rashers

Heat the oven to 200°C, 400°F, gas 6. Cut the leeks into 2.5-cm/1-inch lengths. Scrub and thinly slice the potatoes and chop the celery. Steam the vegetables together for 30 minutes or until they are tender. Cut the ham into 1-cm/½-inch dice. Mix it with the vegetables. Roll out the pastry and use it to line a 25-cm/10-inch square, 5-cm/2-inch deep ovenproof dish. Put in the ham and vegetables. Put the cheese into a bowl with the mustard. Gradually beat in the eggs and mix in the parsley. Pour the mixture over the ham and vegetables. Bake the pie for 10 minutes. Lay the bacon rashers on top and cook for a further 15 minutes, or until the filling is set and beginning to brown. Serve hot or cold.

CAULIFLOWER, CHEESE AND POTATO PIE

1 large cauliflower, about 1 kg/2¼ lb
1 bay leaf
450 g/1 lb potatoes
450 g/1 lb tomatoes
1 tablespoon chopped thyme, or ½ teaspoon
    dried
2 tablespoons chopped parsley
25 g/1 oz butter
2 tablespoons wholewheat flour
2 tablespoons tomato purée
225 ml/8 fl oz stock
150 ml/¼ pint natural yogurt
175 g/6 oz Cheddar cheese, grated
4 eggs, beaten
shortcrust pastry made with 300 g/10 oz
    wholewheat flour

Heat the oven to 200°C, 400°F, gas 6. Break the cauliflower into small florettes. Steam them with the bay leaf for 20 minutes, or until they are just tender. Boil the potatoes in their skins until they are tender and dice them. Scald, skin and chop the tomatoes. Mix together the cauliflower, tomatoes, potatoes and herbs.

Melt the butter in a saucepan on a medium heat. Stir in the flour, tomato purée and stock. Bring them to the boil, stirring. Take the pan from the heat and gradually mix in the yogurt. Simmer, stirring, for 2 minutes, or until the sauce is thick. Take the pan from the heat and beat in all the cheese. Gradually beat in the eggs.

Roll out the pastry and line a 25–cm/10–inch square, 5–cm/2–inch deep ovenproof dish. Put in the vegetables and pour the sauce and egg mixture over the top. Bake the pie for 30 minutes or until the filling is set and golden brown. Serve hot or cold.

CHOUX PASTRY DISHES

A topping of choux pastry is easy to make, and it will make a one-pot meal special and lighter than one made with dumplings or potatoes. The filling often consists of pre-cooked ingredients bound with a sauce.

BROAD BEANS AND FETA CHEESE UNDER CHEESE CHOUX PASTRY

450 g/1 lb shelled broad beans, fresh or frozen
225 g/8 oz feta cheese
25 g/1 oz butter
2 tablespoons wholewheat flour
300 ml/½ pint stock
150 ml/¼ pint single cream
4 tablespoons chopped parsley
1 tablespoon chopped savory, or 1 teaspoon dried

choux pastry
75 g/3 oz butter
225 ml/8 fl oz water
100 g/4 oz wholewheat flour
3 eggs, beaten
75 g/3 oz Cheddar cheese, finely diced

Heat the oven to 200°C, 400°F, gas 6. Cook the beans in lightly salted boiling water for 12 minutes or until tender. Drain them. Finely dice the cheese. Melt the butter in a saucepan on a medium heat. Stir in the flour and then the stock. Bring them to the boil, stirring. Simmer for 2 minutes. Stir in the cream and herbs and take the pan from the heat. Cool the sauce slightly and then fold in the beans and feta cheese.

For the choux pastry, put the butter and water into a saucepan and set them on a medium heat. Bring them to the boil, and when the butter has melted, stir in the flour all at once. Beat until the mixture is smooth and glossy. Take the pan from the heat and cool the mixture for a few minutes. Beat in the eggs, a little at a time. Mix in the cheese.

Put the beans and feta cheese into an ovenproof dish. Spoon or pipe the choux pastry round the edge of the dish, leaving a space in the centre. Put the dish into the oven for 30 minutes, or until the pastry is browned and risen. Serve hot, straight from the dish.

CHICKEN IN RED WINE WITH CHOUX PASTRY

1 small cooked chicken
450 g/1 lb Florence fennel
225 g/8 oz mushrooms
25 g/1 oz butter
1 large onion, finely chopped
2 tablespoons wholewheat flour
300 ml/½ pint stock
150 ml/¼ pint dry red wine
1 tablespoon chopped thyme, or 1 teaspoon
    dried
1 tablespoon chopped marjoram, or 1 teaspoon
    dried

choux pastry
175 g/3 oz butter
225 ml/8 fl oz water
100 g/4 oz wholewheat flour
3 eggs, beaten

Heat the oven to 200°C, 400°F, gas 6. Finely chop all the chicken meat. Chop the fennel and mushrooms. Melt the butter in a saucepan on a low heat. Put in the fennel, mushrooms and onion. Cover them and cook them gently for 10 minutes. Raise the heat to medium. Stir in the flour and then the stock and wine. Bring them to the boil, stirring. Simmer for 2 minutes. Add the herbs and fold in the chicken. Put the contents of the pan into an ovenproof dish.

For the choux pastry, put the butter and water into a saucepan and bring them to the boil on a medium heat. When the butter has melted, stir in the flour all at once and keep stirring until the mixture is smooth. Take the pan from the heat and cool it for a few minutes. Beat in the eggs, a little at a time. Spoon or pipe the choux pastry around the edge of the dish containing the chicken, leaving an open space in the centre. Bake for 30 minutes or until the pastry is risen and golden brown. Serve as soon as possible, straight from the dish.

SALMON UNDER CHOUX PASTRY

2 (200-g/7-oz) cans salmon
350 g/12 oz French beans
225 g/8 oz shelled green peas, fresh or frozen
25 g/1 oz butter
1 small onion, finely chopped
2 tablespoons wholewheat flour
150 ml/¼ pint milk
150 ml/¼ pint dry white wine
4 tablespoons chopped parsley

choux pastry
75 g/3 oz butter
225 ml/8 fl oz water
100 g/4 oz wholewheat flour
4 eggs, beaten

Heat the oven to 200°C, 400°F, gas 6. Drain and flake the salmon. Trim the French beans, break them into 2.5-cm/1-inch pieces and cook them in boiling water for 10 minutes or until they are just tender. Drain them. Cook the peas in boiling water for 10 minutes. Drain them.

Melt the butter in a saucepan on a low heat. Put in the onion and soften it. Raise the heat to medium. Stir in the flour and then the milk. Bring them to the boil, stirring. Add the wine and simmer, stirring frequently, for 2 minutes. Take the pan from the heat and fold in the salmon, beans, peas and parsley. Put the mixture into an ovenproof dish.

For the choux pastry, put the butter and water into a saucepan and bring them to the boil on a medium heat. When the butter has melted, stir in the flour all at once. Beat until the mixture is smooth and glossy. Take the pan from the heat and cool the mixture for a few minutes. Beat in the eggs, a little at a time. Pipe or spoon the mixture in small portions over the salmon. Put the dish into the oven for 30 minutes, or until the pastry is risen and golden brown. Serve hot, straight from the dish.

EGGS AND CORN WITH TOMATO CHOUX PASTRY

6 eggs, hard boiled
2 ripe avocados
25 g/1 oz butter
1 medium onion, finely chopped
2 tablespoons wholewheat flour
2 teaspoons paprika
300 ml/½ pint milk
1 (350-g/12-oz) can sweet corn, drained

choux pastry
75 g/3 oz butter
225 ml/8 fl oz water
2 tablespoons tomato purée
100 g/4 oz wholewheat flour
2 teaspoons paprika
4 eggs, beaten

Heat the oven to 200°C, 400°F, gas 6. Chop the eggs and the avocados. Melt the butter in a saucepan on a low heat. Put in the onion and soften it. Raise the heat to medium. Stir in the flour and paprika and then the milk. Bring them to the boil, stirring. Simmer for 2 minutes. Take the pan from the heat and mix in the eggs, avocados and sweet corn. Put the mixture into an ovenproof dish.

For the choux pastry, put the butter, water and tomato purée into a saucepan. Set them on a medium heat and bring them to the boil. When the butter has melted, stir in the flour all at once and the paprika and stir on the heat until the mixture is smooth and glossy. Take the pan from the heat and cool the mixture for a few minutes. Beat in the eggs, a little at a time. Spoon or pipe the choux pastry over the top of the egg and avocado mixture, in small portions. Put the dish into the oven for 30 minutes, or until the choux pastry is risen and brown. Serve hot, straight from the dish.

RICE AND OTHER GRAINS

Rice is used all over the world to make one-pot meals. Put it into a Chinese stir-fry, a Spanish paella or an Italian risotto. Flavour it with curry or with Middle Eastern spices or combine it with runner beans for a dish with a more British flavour.

The other more unusual grains are all excellent for one-pot meals, and they can all be bought from health food shops. Polenta is an Italian speciality which consists of a thick, corn meal porridge which is cooled, set and sliced and then combined with other ingredients. Corn meal is not corn flour. It is a coarse, yellow flour made from ground whole sweet corn kernels. Like the other grains, it can be bought in health food shops.

CHICKEN WITH RICE AND RUNNER BEANS

one 1.5 kg/3½ lb roasting chicken
450 g/1 lb runner beans
350 g/12 oz carrots
1 large onion
15 g/½ oz butter
2 tablespoons olive or sunflower oil
225 g/8 oz long-grain brown rice
600 ml/1 pint stock
2 teaspoons spiced granular mustard
1 tablespoon chopped savory, or 1 teaspoon dried

Joint the chicken. Slice the beans, dice the carrots and finely chop the onion. Heat the butter and oil together in a large frying pan or sauté pan on a medium heat. Put in the chicken joints, skin side down first. Brown them on both sides and remove them. Lower the heat. Put in the onion and soften it. Stir in the rice, beans and carrots. Pour in the stock and bring it to the boil. Stir in the mustard and savory and replace the chicken. Cover the pan and cook on a low heat for 45 minutes. Serve the chicken on a bed of rice and vegetables.

Note: Suitable for a slow cooker.

SAVOURY PORK AND RICE

675 g/1½ lean pork, from hand, shoulder or leg
2 red peppers
2 green peppers
450 g/1 lb courgettes
2 medium onions
25 g/1 oz lard or butter
2 tablespoons sunflower oil
1 garlic clove, finely chopped
225 g/8 oz long-grain brown rice
2 teaspoons paprika
¼ teaspoon chilli powder
600 ml/1 pint stock

Cut the pork into 2 cm/¾ inch dice. Core and seed the peppers and cut them into strips 2.5 cm × 6 mm/ 1 inch × ¼ inch. Thinly slice the courgettes and the onions. Heat the lard or butter in a large frying pan or sauté pan on a high heat. Put in the pork, brown it and remove it. Lower the heat and add the oil to the pan. Put in the onions and garlic and soften them. Stir in the rice, paprika and chilli powder. Pour in the stock and bring it to the boil. Replace the pork. Cover and simmer for 15 minutes. Put in the peppers and courgettes. Cover again and simmer for 30 minutes, or until both pork and rice are tender.

Note: Suitable for a slow cooker.

MIXED BEAN CASSEROLE

75 g/3 oz red kidney beans, soaked and drained
75 g/3 oz black kidney beans, soaked and
   drained
75 g/3 oz pinto beans, soaked and drained
450 g/1 lb aubergines
1 tablespoon salt
450 g/1 lb courgettes
450 g/1 lb tomatoes
4 tablespoons olive or sunflower oil
2 medium onions, thinly sliced
1 garlic clove, finely chopped
225 g/8 oz long-grain brown rice
600 ml/1 pint stock
300 ml/½ pint tomato and vegetable juice
50 g/2 oz Cheddar cheese, grated
25 g/1 oz dried wholewheat breadcrumbs

Heat the oven to 180°C, 350°F, gas 4. Dice the aubergines. Put them into a collander and sprinkle them with the salt. Leave them to drain for 20 minutes. Rinse them under cold water and dry them with absorbent kitchen paper. Thinly slice the courgettes. Chop the tomatoes.

Heat the oil in a large flameproof casserole on a low heat. Put in the onion and garlic and soften them. Mix in the rice, aubergines, courgettes, tomatoes and beans. Pour in the stock and vegetable juice and bring them to the boil. Cover the casserole and put it into the oven for 1½ hours, or until the beans are soft and most of the liquid has been absorbed.

Mix the cheese and breadcrumbs together and scatter them over the top. Return the casserole to the oven, uncovered, for 15 minutes until the cheese melts and begins to brown. Serve straight from the casserole. Alternatively, transfer the beans to a heatproof serving dish before putting the cheese and breadcrumbs on top.

Note: Suitable for a slow cooker.

ALMOND AND PINEAPPLE STIR-FRY

225 g/8 oz long-grain brown rice
225 g/8 oz almonds
225 g/8 oz carrots
2 green peppers
1 (225-g/8-oz) can bamboo shoots
1 (225-g/8-oz) can water chestnuts
½ medium pineapple
8 spring onions
15 g/½ oz fresh ginger root
4 tablespoons sunflower or groundnut oil
1 garlic clove, finely chopped
4 tablespoons soy sauce

Boil the rice in lightly salted water for 40 minutes, or until it is just tender. Drain it, rinse it with cold water and drain it again. Put the almonds into a shallow pan and cover them with water. Bring them to the boil, drain them and squeeze them from their skins. Slice the carrots very thinly, Core and seed the peppers and cut them into strips 2.5 cm × 6 mm/1 inch × ¼ inch. Thinly slice the bamboo shoots and water chestnuts. Cut the rind and husk from the pineapple and dice the flesh, removing the core. Cut the onions into 2.5-cm/1-inch lengths. Peel and grate the ginger root.

Heat the oil in a wok or large frying pan on a medium heat. Put in the almonds and stir-fry them until they are brown. Remove them. Raise the heat to high. Put in the carrots, peppers, bamboo shoots, water chestnuts, onions, ginger root and garlic and stir-fry for 2 minutes. Add the pineapple and soy sauce and stir-fry for ½ minute. Add the rice and replace the almonds. Stir-fry for 1 minute or until the rice is heated through. Serve as soon as possible.

PORK STIR-FRY

225 g/8 oz long-grain brown rice
450 g/1 lb lean pork belly
4 tablespoons soy sauce
8 spring onions
1 red pepper
½ Chinese cabbage
15 g/½ oz ginger root
4 tablespoons sunflower or groundnut oil
1 garlic clove, finely chopped
175 g/6 oz bean sprouts

Cook the rice in lightly salted boiling water for 40 minutes, or until it is just tender. Drain it, rinse it with cold water and drain again. Cut the pork into small pieces. Put it into a bowl with the soy sauce and leave it for 30 minutes. Cut the spring onions into 2.5-cm/1-inch lengths. Core and seed the pepper and cut it into strips 2.5 cm × 6 mm/1 inch × ¼ inch. Shred the cabbage. Peel and grate the ginger root. Heat the oil in a large wok or frying pan. Put in the pork and garlic. Stir-fry until the pork browns. Put in the onions, pepper, Chinese cabbage and ginger and stir-fry for 2 minutes or until the cabbage just begins to wilt. Add the rice and bean sprouts and stir-fry for a further 2 minutes. Serve as soon as possible.

CURRIED BEEF WITH RICE

675 g/1½ lb lean stewing steak
225 g/8 oz carrots
225 g/8 oz potatoes
1 green pepper
4 green chillies
2 medium onions
4 tablespoons sunflower oil
1 garlic clove, chopped
4 tablespoons curry powder
900 ml/1½ pints stock
225 g/8 oz long-grain brown rice
225 g/8 oz shelled green peas, fresh or frozen
2 tablespoons fresh coriander or parsley

Cut the beef into 2-cm/¾-inch dice. Dice the carrots and potatoes. Core and seed the pepper and cut it into strips 2.5 cm × 6 mm/1 inch × ¼ inch. Core, seed and finely chop the chillies. Thinly slice the onions.

Heat the oil in a large saucepan or flameproof casserole on a high heat. Put in the beef, brown it and remove it. Lower the heat. Mix in the onions, garlic, carrots, potatoes and curry powder. Cook for 2 minutes, stirring frequently. Pour in the stock and bring it to the boil. Replace the beef and add the chillies. Cover and simmer for 30 minutes. Add the rice, pepper and peas. Cover and simmer for 45 minutes, or until both rice and beef are tender. Serve scattered with the fresh coriander or parsley.

Note: Suitable for a slow cooker.

CHICKEN AND SEAFOOD PAELLA

pinch of saffron
2 tablespoons boiling water
100 g/4 oz lean back bacon
4 tablespoons olive oil
4 chicken drumsticks
1 large onion, finely chopped
225 g/8 oz long-grain brown rice
450 ml/¾ pint stock
2 red peppers
2 green peppers
1 (200-g/7-oz) can tuna fish, drained
100 g/4 oz shelled prawns
1 (425-g/15-oz) can asparagus, drained
8 green olives, halved

Infuse the saffron in boiling water for 30 minutes. Chop the bacon. Heat the oil in a paella pan or very large frying pan on a medium heat. Put in the bacon, chicken drumsticks and onion and cook them until the drumsticks are evenly browned. Stir in the rice. Add the stock and infused saffron and bring them to the boil. Cover and simmer for 20 minutes.

Core and seed the peppers and cut them into strips 2.5 cm × 6 mm/1 × ¼ inch. Add them to the pan and continue cooking for a further 25 minutes.

Carefully mix in the tuna, prawns, asparagus and olives. Cover again and cook for 1 minute more. Serve either directly from the pan or transfer the paella to a serving dish.

MUSHROOM AND GREEN BEAN RISOTTO WITH CHEESE

pinch of saffron
2 tablespoons boiling water
225 g/8 oz button mushrooms
450 g/1 lb French beans
1 large onion
50 g/2 oz butter
225 g/8 oz short-grain brown rice
750 ml/1¼ pints stock
175 g/6 oz Mozarella cheese
50 g/2 oz fresh Parmesan cheese

Infuse the saffron in the boiling water for 30 minutes. Thinly slice the mushrooms. Top and tail the beans and cut them into 2.5-cm/1-inch lengths. Finely chop the onion.

Melt the butter in a large saucepan on a low heat. Add the onion and soften it. Add the mushrooms and cook them for 1 minute. Stir in the rice and cook it for 1 minute. Add one-third of the stock and the saffron. Simmer, uncovered, until most of the stock has been absorbed. Add a further third of the stock and simmer again until it has been absorbed. Add the remaining stock and the beans and simmer, uncovered, until the rice is tender and all the stock has been absorbed. Grate the Mozarella and Parmesan cheeses. Fork them into the risotto just before serving.

SPICED LAMB WITH RICE

675 g/1½ lb lean lamb, from leg or shoulder
450 g/1 lb aubergines
1 tablespoon salt
450 g/1 lb courgettes
2 medium onions
4 tablespoons sunflower oil
1 garlic clove, chopped
225 g/8 oz long-grain brown rice
2 teaspoons ground turmeric
2 teaspoons ground coriander
2 teaspoons cumin seeds
¼ teaspoon chilli powder
600 ml/1 pint stock
grated rind and juice of 1 lemon

Cut the lamb into 2.5-cm/¾-inch dice. Dice the aubergines. Put them into a collander and sprinkle them with the salt. Leave them to drain for 20 minutes. Rinse them under cold water. Dry them with absorbent kitchen paper. Slice the courgettes and onions.

Heat the oil in a saucepan or flameproof casserole on a high heat. Put in the lamb, brown it and remove it. Lower the heat. Put in the onions and garlic and soften them. Mix in the aubergines, courgettes, rice and spices. Pour in the stock and bring it to the boil. Replace the lamb and add the lemon rind and juice. Cover and cook gently for 45 minutes, or until both rice and lamb are tender.

Note: Suitable for a slow cooker.

BARLEY CASSEROLE

450 g/1 lb curly kale
225 g/8 oz mushrooms
175 g/6 oz lean back bacon
15 g/½ oz butter
1 large onion, finely chopped
225 g/8 oz pot barley★
600 ml/1 pint stock
freshly ground black pepper
100 g/4 oz Sage Derby cheese, grated

Heat the oven to 180°C, 350°F, gas 4. Tear the kale from the stems and tear it into 2.5-cm/1-inch pieces. Wash and drain it. Thinly slice the mushrooms. Chop the bacon.

Melt the butter in a flameproof casserole on a low heat. Put in the onion and bacon and cook until the onion is soft. Stir in the curly kale, mushrooms and barley. Pour in the stock and bring it to the boil. Season with the pepper. Cover the casserole and put it into the oven for 45 minutes.

Fork in half the cheese and scatter the rest on top. Put the casserole back into the oven, uncovered, for 5 minutes. Serve straight from the casserole. Alternatively, transfer the barley to a heatproof serving dish before adding the cheese.

★Pot barley is whole barley grains without the outer husk removed.

BUCKWHEAT WITH STIR-FRIED SPINACH AND WALNUTS

225 g/8 oz carrots
1 medium onion
450 g/1 lb spinach
225 g/8 oz buckwheat
600 ml/1 pint stock
25 g/1 oz butter
100 g/4 oz chopped walnuts
150 ml/¼ pint double cream
100 g/4 oz Cheddar cheese, grated
2 tablespoons flaked almonds

Heat the oven to 200°C, 400°F, gas 6. Finely chop the carrots, onion and spinach. Heat the buckwheat in a heavy frying pan with no fat, stirring until it begins to brown and smell nutty. Pour in the stock and bring it to the boil. Add the carrots and onion. Cover and cook for 20 minutes or until the buckwheat is soft and all the stock has been absorbed.

Meanwhile, melt the butter in a large frying pan on a high heat. Put in the spinach and stir-fry it for about 3 minutes, or until it has wilted. When the buckwheat is done, mix in the spinach and walnuts. Transfer the mixture to a heatproof serving dish. Mix together the cream and the cheese. Pour them over the buckwheat. Scatter the flaked almonds over the top. Put the dish into the oven for 10 minutes for the almonds to brown and the cheese to melt.

WHEAT WITH STIR-FRIED FISH AND CUCUMBER

675 g/1½ lb cod or haddock fillets
juice of 1 lemon
2 tablespoons olive or sunflower oil
1 medium onion, finely chopped
1 garlic clove, finely chopped
225 g/8 oz burghul wheat
1 (400-g/14-oz) can chopped tomatoes in juice
water to make up 600 ml/1 pint liquid
1 large cucumber
25 g/1 oz butter
2 boxes mustard and cress

Cut the fish into 2-cm/¾-inch pieces. Sprinkle it with half the lemon juice and leave it for 30 minutes.

Heat the oil in a saucepan on a low heat. Put in the onion and garlic and soften them. Stir in the wheat and cook it for ½ minute. Measure the tomatoes and juice together. Make them up to 600 ml/1 pint with water and add them to the wheat. Cover and simmer for 20 minutes, or until the wheat is tender and all the liquid has been absorbed.

Cut the cucumber into 2.5-cm/1-inch sticks. Melt the butter in a large frying pan on a high heat. Put in half the cucumber and stir-fry it for 2 minutes. Add it to the wheat. Stir-fry the remaining cucumber and add it to the wheat. Stir-fry the fish, again in two batches if necessary, so that it just cooks through but does not break up. Mix it carefully into the wheat and add 1 box of mustard and cress. Transfer the wheat and fish to a serving dish and garnish with the remaining mustard and cress.

SPICED MILLET WITH STIR-FRIED CABBAGE, SALAMI AND BEANS

3 tablespoons sunflower oil
1 medium onion, thinly sliced
1 garlic clove, finely chopped
225 g/8 oz millet
2 teaspoons paprika
¼ teaspoon cayenne
600 ml/1 pint stock

for cabbage
1 small white cabbage
100 g/4 oz Italian salami, thinly sliced
4 tablespoons sunflower oil
2 teaspoons paprika
2 tablespoons white wine vinegar
1 (425-g/15-oz) can cannallini beans, drained

Heat the oil in a saucepan on a low heat. Put in the onion and garlic and soften them. Stir in the millet, paprika and cayenne and cook for 1 minute. Pour in the stock and bring it to the boil. Cover and cook gently for 25 minutes or until the millet is soft and fluffy and all the stock absorbed.

Finely shred the cabbage. Quarter the salami slices. Heat the oil in a large frying pan or paella pan on a high heat. Put in the salami and cabbage and stir-fry them for 3 minutes, or until the cabbage has begun to wilt. Sprinkle in the paprika. Add the vinegar and let it bubble. Mix well. Mix in the beans. Fold the cabbage, salami and beans into the millet and transfer to a serving dish.

POLENTA LAYERED WITH MEAT SAUCE AND VEGETABLES

polenta
1.75 litres/3 pints water
1 teaspoon salt
275 g/10 oz corn meal
15 g/½ oz butter

meat sauce
3 tablespoons olive oil
1 medium onion, finely chopped
2 celery sticks, finely chopped
1 medium carrot, finely chopped
1 garlic clove, finely chopped
450 g/1 lb minced beef
2 tablespoons wholewheat flour
2 tablespoons tomato purée
150 ml/¼ pint stock
150 ml/¼ pint dry white wine
1 tablespoon chopped thyme, or 1 teaspoon dried
1 tablespoon chopped marjoram, or 1 teaspoon dried
2 sage leaves, chopped, or ½ teaspoon dried

vegetables
350 g/12 oz carrots
255 g/8 oz French beans

bechamel sauce
40 g/1½ oz butter
3 tablespoons whole-wheat flour
450 ml/¾ pint milk
2 tablespoons grated Parmesan cheese

For the polenta, bring the water to the boil and lower the heat. Add the salt and scatter in the corn meal, stirring. Stir on a low heat for 20 minutes, or until the mixture is thick and porridge-like. Turn the polenta onto greaseproof paper and spread it out to about 2.5 cm/1 inch thick. Leave it for at leat 1 hour to cool completely and set.

For the meat sauce, heat the oil in a saucepan on a low heat. Stir in the onion, celery, carrot and garlic and cook them, uncovered and stirring occasionally, for about 15 minutes, or until they are beginning to brown. Add the beef and stir until it browns. Stir in the flour, tomato purée and stock and bring them to the boil, stirring. Add the wine and herbs. Cover and simmer for 30 minutes.

For the vegetables, thinly slice the carrots and cut the French beans into 2.5-cm/1-inch lengths. Steam them together for 20 minutes or until they are just tender.

For the sauce, melt the butter in a saucepan on a medium heat. Stir in the flour and milk. Bring them to the boil, stirring. Beat in the Parmesan cheese.

Heat the oven to 230°C, 450°F, gas 8. Cut the polenta into 6-mm/¼-inch thick slices. Put one-third of the polenta slices in a single layer in the bottom of a large, deep ovenproof dish. Put in all the meat sauce and cover it with half the bechamel sauce. Put in another one-third of the polenta. Cover it with all the vegetables, and cover these with the remaining bechamel sauce. Finally put on the remaining polenta slices and dot them with the butter. Put the dish into the oven for 10 minutes for the top layer of polenta to brown. Serve straight from the dish.

PASTA

Pasta is quick and easy to cook, is highly versatile and combines well with many different ingredients in one-pot meals which are assembled from prepared ingredients. Both wholewheat pasta and fresh ravioli can be bought in most supermarkets.

PASTA WITH HAM AND MIXED VEGETABLES

225 g/8 oz wholewheat pasta shapes
350 g/12 oz cooked lean ham
350 g/12 oz aubergines
1 tablespoon salt
2 red peppers
2 green peppers
350 g/12 oz tomatoes
1 large onion
4 tablespoons olive or sunflower oil
1 garlic clove, finely chopped

Cook the pasta in lightly salted boiling water for 12 minutes or until just tender. Drain it. Cut the ham into 1-cm/½-inch dice. Dice the aubergines. Put them into a collander and sprinkle them with the salt. Leave them to drain for 20 minutes. Rinse them under cold water and dry them with absorbent kitchen paper. Core and seed the peppers and cut them into strips 2.5 cm × 6 mm/1 × ¼ inch. Scald, skin and chop the tomatoes. Thinly slice the onion. Heat the oil in a saucepan on a low heat. Put in the onion and garlic and cook them for 2 minutes. Mix in the aubergines and peppers. Cover and cook for 10 minutes. Add the tomatoes and ham. Cover and cook for a further 10 minutes. Mix in the pasta and reheat.

PASTA WITH EGGS, SAUSAGE AND FLORENCE FENNEL

225 g/8 oz wholewheat pasta shapes
450 g/1 lb Florence fennel
450 g/1 lb tomatoes
225 g/8 oz chorizo or other similar spiced
   sausage
4 tablespoons olive oil
1 large onion, thinly sliced
1 garlic clove, finely chopped
1 tablespoon chopped thyme, or 1 teaspoon
   dried
2 tablespoons chopped parsley
6 black olives, quartered
4 eggs

Heat the oven to 200°C, 400°F, gas 6. Cook the pasta in lightly salted boiling water for 12 minutes or until just tender. Drain it. Chop the fennel. Chop and reserve the leaves if there are any there. Scald, skin and chop the tomatoes. Thinly slice the sausage. Heat the oil in a frying pan on a low heat. Put in the fennel, sausage, onion and garlic and cook gently, stirring occasionally, until the onion is soft. Add the tomatoes, herbs, olives and chopped fennel leaves and cook for 2 minutes more. Mix in the pasta. Put the mixture into a large, 5-cm/2-inch-deep, oven-proof dish and make 4 indentations in the top with the back of a tablespoon. Carefully break 1 egg into each indentation. Cover the dish with foil and put it into the oven for 20 minutes or until the eggs are set.

PASTA, SPINACH AND TOMATO SCRAMBLE

225 g/8 oz wholewheat pasta shells
450 g/1 lb spinach
8 eggs
100 g/4 oz Cheddar cheese, grated
350 g/12 oz firm tomatoes
40 g/1½ oz butter
1 large onion, thinly sliced
2 teaspoons chopped rosemary, or 1 teaspoon
  dried and crumbled

Cook the pasta in lightly salted boiling water for 12 minutes or until tender. Drain it. Wash the spinach and break off the stems where they meet the leaves. Put the leaves into a saucepan with only the water that clings to them after washing and set them on a low heat for 10 minutes, stirring occasionally. Drain the spinach well, pressing down to extract as much water as possible. Turn it onto a board and chop it finely. Beat the eggs with the cheese. Scald, skin and roughly chop the tomatoes. Melt the butter in a heavy saucepan on a low heat. Add the onion and rosemary and cook them until the onion is golden. Stir in the spinach, egg and cheese mixture and tomatoes. Stir until the eggs are half set. Add the pasta and stir carefully until the eggs are completely set. Serve as soon as possible.

PASTA WITH TUNA FISH, LETTUCE AND CUCUMBER

225 g/8 oz wholewheat pasta shapes
1 large cucumber
1 iceberg lettuce
10 spring onions
3 tablespoons olive oil
2 (200-g/7-oz) cans tuna fish, drained
juice of ½ lemon
4 tablespoons chopped fennel or parsley

Cook the pasta in lightly salted boiling water for 12 minutes or until tender. Drain. Cut the cucumber into lengthways quarters and then into 2.5-cm/1-inch lengths. Shred the lettuce. Cut the onions into 2.5-cm/1-inch lengths. Heat the oil in a saucepan on a low heat. Put in the cucumber and spring onions. Cover and cook them gently for 5 minutes. Mix in the lettuce, pasta, tuna, lemon juice and fennel or parsley. Shake the pan to heat them through. Serve as soon as possible.

TWO-LAYER VEGETABLE LASAGNE

225 g/8 oz wholewheat lasagne
450 g/1 lb carrots
225 g/8 oz mushrooms
75 g/3 oz watercress
2 medium onions
50 g/2 oz butter or vegetable margarine
1 garlic clove, finely chopped
4½ tablespoons wholewheat flour
600 ml/1 pint milk
1 teaspoon mild spiced granular mustard
2 boxes mustard and cress
1 teaspoon Dijon mustard
125 g/4 oz Cheddar cheese, grated

Heat the oven to 200°C, 400°F, gas 6. Cook the lasagne in lightly salted boiling water for 12 minutes or until tender. Drain it, run cold water through it and drain it again. Grate the carrots. Finely chop the mushrooms, watercress and onions.

Melt one-third of the butter in a saucepan on a low heat. Stir in the carrots, one of the onions and the garlic clove. Cover and cook gently for 10 minutes. Stir in 1½ tablespoons flour and one-third of the milk. Bring to the boil, stirring, and stir until the carrots are coated with a small amount of thick sauce. Take the pan from the heat. Stir in the granular mustard. Cut the mustard and cress from the boxes and fold it into the carrot mixture.

Melt a further third of the butter in a saucepan on a low heat. Put in the remaining onion and soften it. Raise the heat to medium. Put in the mushrooms and cook them for 1½ minutes, stirring frequently. Stir in 1½ tablespoons of flour and a further third of the milk. Bring to the boil, stirring, and stir until you have a thick sauce. Take the pan from the heat and beat in one-third of the cheese and all the watercress.

Melt the remaining butter in a saucepan on a medium heat. Stir in the remaining flour and milk and bring them to the boil. Simmer for 2 minutes. Beat in half the remaining cheese and the Dijon mustard.

In a large 5-to-8-cm/2-to-3-inch-deep dish, place one-third of the lasagne. Cover it with all the carrot mixture. Arrange a further third of the lasagne on top. Cover this layer with the mushroom and watercress mixture. Top with the remaining lasagne and spread the cheese sauce over it. Sprinkle the remaining grated cheese on top. Bake the lasagne for 30 minutes, or until the top is golden brown.

TORTELLONI WITH CHICORY

450 g/1 lb chicory
450 g/1 lb tomatoes
4 tablespoons olive oil
1 large onion, thinly sliced
1 garlic clove, finely chopped
2 tablespoons chopped basil, or 1 teaspoon dried
1 tablespoon chopped thyme or ½ teaspoon dried
1 tablespoon chopped marjoram, or ½ teaspoon dried
450 g/1 lb fresh tortelloni
4 tablespoons chopped parsley

Thinly slice the chicory. Scald, skin and chop the tomatoes. Heat the oil in a large saucepan on a low heat. Put in the onion and garlic and soften them.

Mix in the chicory, tomatoes, basil, thyme, marjoram and tortelloni. Cover and cook on a low heat for 12 minutes, or until the tortelloni is tender. Serve scattered with parsley.

Note: Ravioli may be used instead of tortelloni.

SALADS

Salads are not often associated with one-pot meals, yet a salad, too, can combine all the ingredients of a balanced meal in one dish, even though, in most cases, no cooking is involved. One-pot salads are suitable for light lunch and supper dishes.

BEAN, CORN AND PASTA SALAD

225 g/8 oz wholewheat pasta shapes
450 g/1 lb French beans
225 g/8 oz button mushrooms
100 g/4 oz red kidney beans, soaked and cooked
100 g/4 oz pinto beans, soaked and cooked
1 (350-g/12-oz) can sweet corn kernels, drained
4 tablespoons olive oil
2 tablespoons white wine vinegar
½ teaspoon dried thyme
1 garlic clove, crushed

Cook the pasta in lightly salted boiling water for 12 minutes, or until tender. Drain it, rinse it with cold water and drain it again. Break the French beans into 2.5-cm/1-inch lengths. Cook them in lightly salted boiling water for 10 minutes. Drain and cool them. Thinly slice the mushrooms. Combine all these ingredients with the kidney beans, pinto beans and corn. Beat the remaining ingredients together to make the dressing and fold it into the salad.

WHEAT, WALNUT AND CELERY SALAD

225 g/8 oz burghul wheat
175 g/6 oz shelled walnuts
6 large celery sticks
2 small dessert apples
2 ripe avocados
1 green pepper
4 tablespoons olive oil
2 tablespoons cider vinegar
1 garlic clove, crushed
freshly ground black pepper

Soak the wheat in warm water for 20 minutes. Drain it and squeeze it dry. Chop the walnuts. Chop the celery sticks. Core and chop the apples. Peel and dice the avocados. Core, seed and chop the pepper. Combine all these with the wheat and walnuts. Beat the remaining ingredients together to make the dressing. Fold them into the salad.

TAGLIATELLE, SAUSAGE AND BUTTER BEAN SALAD

225 g/8 oz green tagliatelle
225 g/8 oz Frankfurter sausages
350 g/12 oz tomatoes
100 g/4 oz butter beans, soaked and cooked, or
    1 (425-g/15-oz) can butter beans, drained
3 boxes mustard and cress
4 tablespoons olive oil
2 tablespoons white wine vinegar
1 teaspoon German mustard
1 garlic clove, crushed

Cook the tagliatelle in lightly salted boiling water for 12 minutes, or until tender. Drain it, run cold water through it and drain again. Cool completely. Thinly slice the sausages. Scald, skin and chop the tomatoes. Combine these with the tagliatelle and beans. Cut in the mustard and cress. Beat the remaining ingredients together to make the dressing and fold it into the salad.

RICE AND SMOKED MACKEREL SALAD

225g/8 oz long-grain brown rice
350 g/12 oz smoked mackerel fillets
225 g/8 oz chicory
225 g/8 oz tomatoes
1 large orange
2 pickled dill cucumbers
4 tablespoons olive oil
2 tablespoons white wine vinegar
1 teaspoon paprika
pinch of cayenne

Cook the rice in lightly salted boiling water until tender, about 40 minutes. Drain it, rinse it with cold water and drain it again. Flake the mackerel. Thinly slice the chicory. Chop the tomatoes. Cut the rind and pith from the orange and chop the flesh. Finely chop the cucumbers. Combine all these in a salad bowl. Beat the remaining ingredients together to make the dressing and fold them into the salad.

INDEX